Original title:
The Inner Awakening

Copyright © 2024 Book Fairy Publishing
All rights reserved.

Author: Claudia Kuma
ISBN HARDBACK: 978-9916-87-064-8
ISBN PAPERBACK: 978-9916-87-065-5

The Call Within

In silence deep, the whispers rise,
A gentle pull, where courage lies.
The heartbeats echo, a steady drum,
A voice inside, it's time to come.

Through shadows cast, the path unfolds,
With every step, a truth retold.
The stars above, they shimmer bright,
Guiding souls through darkest night.

The dreams we hold, like fragile glass,
Reflecting futures, as moments pass.
They dance and twirl, they bend and sway,
A call to chase the light of day.

In every beat, in every breath,
The call within defies all death.
Embrace the fire, let it ignite,
For in our hearts, we find our light.

So heed the voice, let passions soar,
A journey starts, forevermore.
Trust the call, let it begin,
For life awaits, the call within.

Chasing the Inner Light

In shadows deep, we search for glow,
A flicker bright, a seed to sow.
Through tangled thoughts and whispered fears,
We turn our gaze, the path appears.

With every step, the darkness fades,
Illuminated, the heart invades.
We chase the spark, our souls alight,
Together journey, towards the bright.

The silence calls, a gentle guide,
Through storms of doubt, we will not hide.
For every dream, a light to find,
In every heart, a thread aligned.

In morning's glow, new hope ascends,
The inner light, as time transcends.
We hold the flame, with steady grace,
A dance of life, our sacred space.

The Silent Symphony

In quiet hours, the music plays,
A symphony that gently sways.
With notes of peace, we breathe the sound,
In silence, beauty can be found.

Each rustle leaves, a whispered song,
Where stillness thrives, we all belong.
The heartbeat soft, a rhythmic flow,
In cozy corners, love will grow.

Beyond the noise, within the calm,
The sacred notes, a soothing balm.
In shadows cast by moonlit nights,
We find the truth in subtle sights.

Together still, the world falls mute,
With nature's hymn, we take root.
A melody that never ends,
In every heart, the silence blends.

Rebirth of the Spirit

As seasons change, the spirit wakes,
From winter's grasp, the dawn remakes.
In blooms anew, we find our grace,
A tender touch, a warm embrace.

The past retreats, a lesson learned,
With every flame, the passion burned.
In ashes lies the strength to rise,
A clearer view, with open eyes.

The winds of change, they fill the sails,
As courage flows, the doubt unveils.
With every step, the heart expands,
In unity, we join our hands.

The spirit soars, a joyous flight,
Through valleys low, into the light.
In every heartbeat, life reborn,
With hope and love, we greet the morn.

The Awakening Path

Beneath the stars, the journey calls,
A winding way, where darkness falls.
With every choice, a door swings wide,
In every moment, we must decide.

The whispers soft, they guide the way,
Through trials faced, we learn to stay.
With wisdom gained, we rise and shine,
In every struggle, strength divine.

Through tangled roots, we find our ground,
In nature's arms, the truth is found.
With open hearts, we tread the trail,
In unity, we shall not fail.

As dawn emerges, hope ignites,
A path of dreams, where love unites.
With courage held, we walk the song,
In every step, we all belong.

A Journey Within

In silence deep, I close my eyes,
Waves of thoughts begin to rise.
Echoes of dreams softly call,
In this space, I seek it all.

Footprints traced on paths unknown,
Whispers guide where seeds are sown.
Mirrors reflect my hidden fears,
With each breath, dissolve my tears.

Mountains high and valleys wide,
Inward bound, I turn the tide.
Lessons carved in inner stone,
Newfound strength, I make it known.

Through tangled roots, I find my way,
Beneath the stars, I choose to stay.
Guided by a heart that's free,
This journey's mine, a soul's decree.

Unraveled Thoughts

Threads of mind begin to part,
Woven tales of a restless heart.
In the chaos, clarity grows,
As I sift through what I know.

Each memory, a fragile piece,
Crafting sense, a slow release.
Insights dance like swirling leaves,
In every turn, the spirit heaves.

Questions linger in the night,
Flickering dim, yet shining bright.
Fragments float like autumn skies,
In the quiet, truth underlies.

With every thought, a thread I find,
Patterns weave, a sacred bind.
In the depths, I trace the lines,
Unraveled thoughts, where wisdom shines.

Seeds of Self-Discovery

Tiny seeds in fertile ground,
Within my heart, a truth is found.
Watered with care, they start to grow,
Roots that reach where rivers flow.

Each blossom sings a gentle tune,
In the light of the warming moon.
With every petal, hope unfolds,
Awakening dreams, like stories told.

Sunlight dapples, shadows play,
In nature's dance, I find my way.
Seasons change, yet I remain,
Nurtured by both joy and pain.

Harvest time brings treasures new,
Lessons learned, perspectives too.
Within these seeds, the call is clear,
To honor self, and shed the fear.

Flashes of Clarity

In silence, thoughts collide,
Wisps of truth arrive,
Shattered doubts dissolve,
A spark begins to thrive.

Moments bright and rare,
Guiding through the mist,
With every glowing flare,
A gentle healer's kiss.

Waves of insight surge,
A tide of pure intent,
In this sacred urge,
Wisdom's voice is pent.

Light breaks through the gray,
Illumination's grace,
Each step a dawning ray,
Within this timeless space.

As clarity takes form,
In shadows cast by doubt,
A new vision is born,
A mind that dares to shout.

The Breath of Clarity

Inhale deeply, feel the flow,
Each breath a gift, a chance to grow.
Exhale softly, release the weight,
Find your center, don't hesitate.

Moments pause like rippling waves,
Within the stillness, the spirit saves.
Guided by the pulse of life,
Embrace the calm, dismiss the strife.

Mind unwinds like threads of gold,
Wisdom spoken, truth retold.
In every breath, a sacred chance,
To weave tranquility in the dance.

Through layers deep, my heart beats clear,
In this space, I shed my fear.
The breath of clarity flows free,
Awakening the soul in me.

Storms of Clarity

In thunder's roar, we find our voice,
The heart lays bare, no hidden choice.
Lightning strikes with vivid light,
Revealing truths obscured by night.

The winds of change begin to blow,
As fears dissolve, we start to grow.
Through tempest's rage, we learn to stand,
Embracing all we had not planned.

With rain that falls, we wash away,
The doubts that kept our dreams at bay.
In chaos found, a strength untold,
We rise anew, tenacious, bold.

When storm has passed, the calm returns,
In silence, now the spirit yearns.
For clarity that comes in strife,
A clearer path, our truest life.

The Quiet Revolution

In whispers low, the change does stir,
A subtle shift, like breeze in fur.
With every heart, a spark ignites,
In gentle acts, the future writes.

No banners raised, nor cries of war,
Just love and peace, and so much more.
In quiet rooms, the plans unfold,
A tapestry of courage bold.

The strength of souls, a force unseen,
In silent moments, we glean.
With every step, the ground will tremble,
Roots intertwine as we assemble.

Together we mold, reshape the dream,
The quiet change, a flowing stream.
In unity, our voices blend,
A revolution that won't end.

Whispers of the Soul

In twilight hues, our spirits speak,
With gentle nudges, soft and meek.
In silence loud, the truth reveals,
The heart's deep longings, what it feels.

Each whisper thougth, a guiding light,
Illuminates the darkest night.
Within the calm, we sense the grace,
Of timeless love in every space.

With echoes rich, the visions flow,
From depths unknown, where secrets grow.
In tranquil moments, wisdom shines,
And every breath, the soul aligns.

When listening close, the world unfolds,
In quietude, the heart beholds.
These whispers true, forever stay,
As we embark on our own way.

Inward Journeys

In shadows deep, we dive within,
To face the fears, to shed the skin.
With every step, a world awaits,
Unlocking hearts, unlocking gates.

The paths we tread, though rough and long,
Are woven tight, like ancient song.
Each moment passed, a lesson learned,
With every flicker, a flame is burned.

Through valleys low, and mountains high,
We seek the truth, we aim to fly.
In stillness found, our spirits soar,
Inward journeys lead us to more.

With every breath, a chance to grow,
To find the light in all we know.
Embrace the quest, the path ahead,
In inward journeys, we are led.

The Heart's Prism

Through the prism of the heart,
Colors blend and dance,
Each hue a work of art,
In love's enchanting trance.

Radiant shades unfold,
Stories in their glow,
Warmth in every fold,
As feelings come to show.

Fragile beams of light,
Breaking day from night,
In the still twilight,
Hope takes silent flight.

Every tear and laugh,
Reflections we embrace,
In this vibrant path,
We find our rightful place.

When shadows linger near,
The prism holds its ground,
With love we persevere,
In colors, joy is found.

Unfolding Wisdom

In the quiet of dawn's embrace,
Thoughts awaken, begin to trace.
Pages of life, stories unfold,
In whispers soft, the truth is told.

Morning light on aged trees,
Rustles secrets in the breeze.
Every stillness holds a key,
Unlocking what we long to see.

Lessons learned from paths we've crossed,
Each moment cherished, never lost.
With every tear, and every laugh,
We carve our way, we sketch our path.

The heart's a sage with boundless grace,
In trials faced, we find our place.
Perspective shifts, revealing sights,
Both shadowed truths and radiant lights.

Wisdom blooms in gentle hands,
Like fertile ground in sunlit lands.
Embrace the journey, feel its beat,
In every step, find love complete.

Steps of the Unseen

In moonlit nights, we wander far,
Tracing dreams beneath the star.
Paths that twist, yet gently guide,
Through realms where mysteries reside.

The shadows dance with tales untold,
Echoes linger, brave and bold.
With silent prayers, we seek and yearn,
For the lessons that we learn.

Each footfall whispers of the past,
A tapestry of shadows cast.
Through thickets thick and valleys deep,
Our spirits soar, our secrets keep.

Navigating through the haze,
Life's fine threads weave in a maze.
Unseen forces at play around,
In hidden depths, the truth is found.

With eyes closed tight, we find our way,
Guided by the heart's soft sway.
In every breath, the unseen calls,
Awakening life, where darkness falls.

Luminescent Pathways

Lights that shimmer on misty trails,
Guiding lanterns through winds and gales.
Each step aglow with hope's sweet spark,
Illuminating paths so dark.

The journey weaves through twisted lanes,
Where joy and sorrow leave their stains.
Bright reflections of all we've known,
In every light, a seed is sown.

Stars above whisper dreams to chase,
Mapping out our sacred space.
With every heartbeat, the world aligns,
In radiant shades, our purpose shines.

Through shadows deep, our spirits rise,
Bathed in light beneath the skies.
With courage found in brimming hearts,
Together we play our destined parts.

As night gives way to dawn's embrace,
We hold the light, we find our place.
On luminescent pathways, we tread,
Illuminating steps where none have led.

Mapping the Unknown

In corners dark, we chart the way,
With every doubt, we learn to sway.
A compass made of hope and trust,
Guides us forth, igniting lust.

Rivers bend, and mountains rise,
Through uncharted lands, our spirit flies.
The canvas stretched, our hands prepare,
To paint our dreams upon the air.

Each adventure calls, a siren's song,
In the heart's echo, we belong.
Mapping dreams in lines unseen,
Where courage blooms, and fears are gleaned.

With every map, we seek a core,
Finding treasures on an endless shore.
In the heart of chaos, we may find,
The beauty born of the unrefined.

As stars align in skies so grand,
We write our tales, and take a stand.
Mapping the unknown, bold and free,
In every step, our destiny.

Rebirth of the Spirit

From ashes rise the hopes anew,
A flame ignites, a path breaks through.
Embrace the light, let shadows flee,
In this soft dawn, we find the key.

Wings stretch wide, the heart takes flight,
In every whisper, a spark of light.
The soul rejuvenates, a vibrant hue,
With every heartbeat, life feels true.

Through trials faced, the strength will grow,
A garden blooms where courage flows.
Renewed in spirit, we stand as one,
With every dawn, a new day begun.

Let go the past, the burdens shed,
Awake with dreams where hope is fed.
The journey calls, the world awaits,
In every moment, the spirit creates.

Fragments of a Dream

Whispers dance in twilight's gleam,
A tapestry of a distant dream.
Colors blend in the dusky light,
Awakening thoughts of endless night.

Fleeting moments slip from grasp,
Like grains of sand in memories clasp.
Stars twinkle with their silent grace,
Each one holds a hidden place.

In visions lost, yet sweetly found,
Echoes of laughter, a shimmering sound.
Fragments weave through the mind's embrace,
Chasing shadows, a timeless chase.

Dreams unfold like petals wide,
In every heart, they take their ride.
A glimpse of joy in softest sighs,
A world reborn as sleep complies.

Lighthouses in the Dark

Amidst the storm, a beacon stands,
Guiding souls with gentle hands.
Illuminated paths through shadows deep,
A promise made, a vow to keep.

In darkest nights, their brilliance shines,
Casting hope through tangled pines.
Each flicker whispers strength to find,
In the heart's depth, a light unconfined.

Through waves that crash and tempests rage,
These lighthouses become the stage.
With steadfast resolve, they light the way,
Transforming chaos into a new day.

Horizon glows as dawn breaks clear,
A harbinger of dreams held dear.
In every heart, a lighthouse gleams,
Filling the dark with golden beams.

Colors of the Unexplored

Vivid shades in distant lands,
A canvas bright that nature brands.
Each hue a tale, each tone a song,
In the unknown, we find where we belong.

Mountains rise in purples bold,
A treasure box of stories told.
Rivers weave with emerald grace,
Connecting hearts in a wondrous space.

The skies blush pink at sunset's kiss,
In every shade, a world of bliss.
Color spills where dreams ignite,
In silence speaks the pure delight.

Fields of gold in the morning light,
Remind us of the beauty in sight.
Uncharted lands await our roam,
In every color, we find our home.

Vibrations of Inner Silence

In the quiet, a soft hum,
Thoughts like ripples gently come.
Moments suspended, time stands still,
In this space, we find our will.

Whispers echo, deep and low,
Carried high, where wind does blow.
Voices of the heart arise,
In silence, our spirit flies.

A dance of shadows, light in trance,
In stillness, we take our chance.
Every heartbeat, a gentle tide,
In the silence, we confide.

Layers of calm, a soothing balm,
Amidst the chaos, we find calm.
The pulse of life, a rhythmic song,
In this stillness, we belong.

Awakening, the soul's delight,
Vibrations flow, pure and bright.
As we listen to the near,
Inner silence draws us near.

Midnight Musings

Underneath the stars,
Thoughts begin to weave,
In the night's soft bars,
I wander and believe.

Shadows play their game,
Whispers touch the ground,
Each spark feels the same,
In night's embrace, I'm found.

Dreams twinkle like lights,
In the velvet sky,
Breathing in the sights,
As time drifts by.

Moments deep and vast,
Captured in the still,
As echoes of the past,
Wrap around my will.

In midnight's calm grace,
The world fades away,
Leaving a soft trace,
Of thoughts meant to stay.

Spheres of Insight

In the cosmos, wisdom swirls,
A dance of thoughts, like pearls.
Each sphere holds a truth to share,
An echo of the soul's own care.

Guided by the stars above,
We seek the light, we seek the love.
In spheres of thought, we explore wide,
Illuminated by the guide.

With every turn, a new embrace,
Hidden paths, a sacred space.
The universe, a vast expanse,
Invites us all to take a chance.

In stillness found among the spheres,
We melt away our doubts and fears.
For insight flows like rivers wide,
In each moment, we abide.

Across the realms, our spirits soar,
Unlocking every hidden door.
Through the spheres, we intertwine,
In realms of insight, we align.

Whispers in the Silence

Amidst the hush, we start to hear,
Soft whispers drawing us near.
The tales unfold, a gentle breeze,
In silence, mysteries appease.

Echoes dance on twilight's edge,
In the shadows, we make a pledge.
To listen closely to the still,
In the silence, we find our thrill.

Every breath carries a story,
In quietude, there's hidden glory.
Weaving threads of thought so fine,
In every pause, wisdom's sign.

The subtle sounds of nature call,
In stillness, we can feel it all.
Whispers linger, soft and clear,
In the silence, we persevere.

As night enfolds, the stars align,
Within the silence, our hearts entwine.
Each whisper, a guiding light,
In darkness, we find insight.

The Depths of Reflection

In still waters, truth does flow,
Calm reflections gently show.
Diving deep into the core,
In silence, we seek to explore.

Moments linger, deep and vast,
Connecting threads from future to past.
The depths we brave unveil our soul,
Each gaze within makes us whole.

Mirrors of truth in shadows cast,
Lessons hidden, wisdom amassed.
Through every ripple, thoughts arise,
In stillness, we seek what lies.

The heart's journey, a winding road,
In reflective depths, we unload.
With each insight, a newfound grace,
In the depths, we find our place.

As we ponder, the layers peel,
Every moment, a chance to heal.
In the depths, we meet the light,
In reflection, we take flight.

The Silent Beneath

In shadows deep where whispers dwell,
The silent songs begin to swell.
A world unseen, yet ever near,
Embracing all that we hold dear.

Here secrets hide in soft embrace,
Each heartbeat paints a sacred space.
Beneath the waves, the stillness flows,
In quiet depths, the spirit grows.

The language of the heart is clear,
In silence speaks what we hold dear.
A harmony both sweet and vast,
Remembering the ancient past.

With every breath, a timeless thread,
A tapestry of words unsaid.
We find our strength beneath the weight,
In silent love, we learn our fate.

So listen close, let go of haste,
For in the quiet, dreams are traced.
The silent song forever sings,
A lullaby of hidden wings.

Awakened Vibrations

The morning breaks with colors bold,
Awakened dreams in hues of gold.
Each note that dances on the breeze,
Invites our hearts to move with ease.

In every strum, in every beat,
A pulse of life, a rhythm sweet.
The world ignites with vibrant light,
As shadows fade into the night.

The energy in every space,
Awakens joy, ignites our grace.
We tune ourselves to nature's song,
Where all our doubts can't linger long.

Embrace the waves, let worries flee,
In this connection, we are free.
With open hearts, we feel the flow,
Awakened souls begin to glow.

So dance beneath the sky so wide,
And let the music be your guide.
As vibrations rise, we soar above,
In harmony, we find our love.

Beyond the Mirror

Reflections hold a twisted tale,
In glass we seek, yet often fail.
What lies beyond the surface bright?
A deeper truth without the light.

In every glance, a fleeting sigh,
The layers peel, we wonder why.
The mirror speaks, yet hides the scars,
Revealing dreams, just like the stars.

Peering in, what do we see?
A glimpse of self, a destiny.
Behind the veil, a heart's desire,
Yearning for truths that never tire.

To seek the essence, pure and rare,
Beyond the mask, beyond despair.
With every crack, a story grows,
In shattered light, the spirit glows.

So dare to look, to face the loss,
Embrace the journey, bear the cross.
For in the depths, we come alive,
Beyond the mirror, we will thrive.

Guided by Inner Stars

Amidst the night, the cosmos gleams,
A tapestry woven with our dreams.
Each star a beacon in the dark,
Illuminating paths we embark.

With gentle whispers, the stars align,
Guiding souls with love divine.
In silent gaze, we find our way,
Where hopes ignite and spirits sway.

The universe calls, a tender guide,
Through every challenge, we abide.
Each shining orb, a truth revealed,
In cosmic light, our fate is sealed.

So let your heart reach for the skies,
For in their glow, the answer lies.
With every breath, a spark ignites,
In starlit dreams, our spirit writes.

Together we roam through endless nights,
A journey blessed by magical sights.
Guided by stars that always shine,
In their embrace, forever divine.

Heartbeats of the Universe

In the quiet night we listen,
Stars whisper secrets, so bright.
Galaxies twirl with gentle grace,
Each heartbeat echoes, pure delight.

Time dances softly, in and out,
Every moment a fleeting spark.
We chase the shadows, hold the light,
To find our way through the dark.

Waves of stardust, dreams collide,
Their rhythm flows in cosmic streams.
Planets spin in silent waltz,
As we awake from timeless dreams.

In the silence, a heartbeat plays,
The pulse of life, a guiding song.
Every echo a truth revealed,
In the universe, we all belong.

So let us dance beneath the stars,
With every heartbeat, we are one.
The universe in our embrace,
Together beneath the sun.

The Labors of Introspection

In the silence of our minds,
Questions linger, shadows creep.
Every thought a winding road,
In the depths of dreams we steep.

Reflections swirl, a mirror's gaze,
Truths we face, both dark and light.
Peeling layers, one by one,
Seeking wisdom, seeking sight.

The heart's voice whispers quietly,
In the chaos, find your peace.
Through the storms of turbulent thoughts,
Let the inner battle cease.

With every breath, a chance to grow,
To weave the threads of self anew.
In the tapestry of human soul,
Each labor creates the view.

And as we travel through the dark,
A light emerges, soft and fair.
The labor of introspection,
Leads to love, to self-care.

Keeper of the Inner Light

Deep within, a flame resides,
A flicker fierce, a beacon bright.
In the darkness, it will guide,
The keeper of the inner light.

Through the valleys, we may roam,
Searching for paths that feel like home.
With every step, the light will shine,
A compass true, a force divine.

When doubts arise, and shadows play,
Remember the warmth, let fear decay.
For you are strong, and you are free,
The keeper holds eternity.

In quiet moments, breathe it in,
The inner flame, where truth begins.
Let love ignite, let hope ignite,
Be the keeper of your light.

So stand tall, let courage reign,
In your heart, no room for pain.
For as you shine, the world can see,
The beauty of your authenticity.

Blossoms of Awakening

In the garden of the soul,
Petals bloom with vibrant grace.
Each blossom tells a story,
Of transformation, time, and space.

Spring arrives with gentle hands,
Awakening dreams long asleep.
Through cracks of doubt, a flower grows,
In its beauty, secrets keep.

Raindrops fall, a soft embrace,
Nourishing roots deep within.
With sunlight's kiss, they rise anew,
Life's circle starts again.

Every petal, a chance to learn,
In the dance of joy and strife.
Embrace the change, let go the past,
And celebrate this wondrous life.

So let your spirit blossom bright,
As seasons shift, and moments sway.
In the garden of awakening,
Find your voice, come what may.

The Quest for Essence

In shadows deep, we search for light,
A whisper calls in the dead of night.
With hearts afire, we stare ahead,
Chasing the dreams that dance like thread.

We wander paths both strange and new,
Through valleys wide, 'neath skies so blue.
In every turn, a lesson learned,
As passion's flame within us burned.

Each step we take is draped in hope,
With every stumble, we learn to cope.
The essence found within our soul,
Is the truest part that makes us whole.

Through trials faced, we rise and stand,
United strong, we join our hand.
Together onward, we shall stride,
In quest of essence, side by side.

In the end, it's not the gold,
But every tale, each truth retold.
For in this quest, we find the key,
The essence lives in you and me.

Celestial Reflections

Beneath the stars, we seek our place,
In vast expanse, we find our grace.
Galaxies bloom, in silent dance,
A cosmic waltz, a fleeting chance.

The moonlight glimmers on the sea,
A mirror shows what's meant to be.
In depths of night, our thoughts take flight,
As dreams emerge, so bold, so bright.

Constellations whisper tales of old,
Of heroes brave and hearts of gold.
We search for meaning in the gleam,
In shadows cast, we chase our dream.

Reflections deep, they stir within,
An inner voice, above the din.
The universe, vast and wide,
In its embrace, we shall abide.

With every glance at heaven's dome,
We find the path that leads us home.
For in the stars, our spirits blend,
A cosmic bond that knows no end.

Breathing Life into Dreams

In whispered hopes, the visions bloom,
From silent cries in the darkest room.
With each beat, our aspirations rise,
As we breathe life into the skies.

Every heartbeat drums a new refrain,
A symphony born from joy and pain.
In shadows cast, we fiercely fight,
To turn our dreams into pure light.

In gardens grown from seeds of trust,
We tend our passions, strong and just.
With hands of toil, and hearts aflame,
We carve our path, and stake our claim.

Through trials faced, our spirits soar,
With every breath, we yearn for more.
For dreams are wings that help us fly,
In boundless realms, we touch the sky.

So let us dance in the moon's glow,
As vibrant tales of life unfold.
Breathing life into dreams we chase,
Together, we create our space.

Huddled Within

In quiet corners, time stands still,
We gather whispers, hearts to fill.
Huddled close, we share the night,
In the warmth of hope, we find our light.

With stories spun like golden thread,
In every word, a life is led.
Through laughter shared and tears we've shed,
A tapestry of love is spread.

Embracing all, both joy and pain,
In the stormy skies, we lose the rain.
Together strong, we face the cold,
With every moment, memories bold.

The world outside may roar and wail,
But within our hearts, we shall not fail.
For in this bond, our spirits rise,
Huddled within, we touch the skies.

And when the dawn breaks through the haze,
We'll greet the sun with hearty praise.
For in this circle, we have grown,
A family found, a love we've sown.

Untold Stories of the Spirit

In whispers soft and clear,
Stories wait to be told,
Echoes of the dear,
Footprints made of gold.

Hidden in the breeze,
Secrets gently sway,
Through the rustling trees,
They speak in their own way.

The moonlight knows our tales,
A dance in silver light,
In night's quiet veils,
Our spirits take to flight.

Fading like a dream,
Yet vivid in the soul,
With every silent scream,
We grasp to feel whole.

These stories intertwine,
A tapestry of grace,
Each thread by design,
In time's warm embrace.

The Quest for Authenticity

In a world of masks we wear,
Truth hides, elusive, rare.
With every step we seek the light,
To find ourselves, to take flight.

Voices echo, doubts persist,
In the shadows, we resist.
Yet within lies a spark so bright,
Guiding with its gentle light.

Paths unfold, choices to make,
With each choice, new bonds we stake.
To be real is to be brave,
Embrace the waves, let us rave.

Layers shed, the soul laid bare,
Finding freedom in the air.
The quest begins – just one more stride,
With open hearts, let truth reside.

In the end, it's clear to see,
Authenticity sets us free.
Through trials faced, we come to know,
The beauty of our inner glow.

Breath of the Unseen

Whispers dance on gentle breeze,
Carrying dreams among the trees.
In the silence, secrets swell,
Stories only nature can tell.

Eyes may wander, hearts will yearn,
For the lessons that we learn.
In every shadow, in every ray,
Lies the breath of life at play.

Mountains high and rivers deep,
Hold the wisdom we must keep.
In the echoes of the night,
The unseen comes to bring delight.

Feel the pulse of earth's sweet song,
In its rhythm, we belong.
Let it guide you, let it flow,
In its arms, we learn to grow.

The unseen world, a tender grace,
Awakens in each sacred space.
Through gentle breath, we come to see,
The magic that sets our spirits free.

Whispered Truths

In the quiet of the night,
Whispers carry soft and light.
Secrets shared among the stars,
Lifting hearts to heal their scars.

Emotions held within our souls,
Yearn for words to make us whole.
Through the murmur, trust is born,
From the shadows, hope is drawn.

Listen closely, feel the air,
Each whisper says that we care.
In the stillness, truths unfold,
Stories waiting to be told.

Let the whispers guide your way,
In their warmth, you'll find your sway.
For in sharing, bonds we weave,
In whispered truths, we all believe.

Together, let our voices blend,
Through whispered truths, we start to mend.
A tapestry of heartfelt dreams,
Bound by love, or so it seems.

Awakening the Stillness

In the hush of dawn,
The world feels reborn.
Soft whispers in the air,
Awake without a care.

Gentle breezes sway,
Beneath the light of day.
Moments held so tight,
Embrace the morning light.

With each breath we take,
The past starts to break.
In silence, we find peace,
A calm that will not cease.

Nature's lullaby plays,
Guiding through the maze.
Each leaf, a soft sigh,
Underneath the vast sky.

Awakened and aware,
We find solace there.
In stillness, we grow,
And let our hearts flow.

Blossoming from Within

From the depths, a bud appears,
Nurtured by hopes and fears.
In the silence, roots take hold,
Blossoming, life's story told.

Sunlight dances on the leaves,
In every sigh, the spirit breathes.
Through the darkness, colors shine,
A miracle, pure and divine.

Each petal soft, each scent a sigh,
Whispers of the earth and sky.
In this heart, a garden grows,
True beauty in the love it sows.

Seasons change, yet still we bloom,
Transforming shadows into room.
With open hearts, we learn to live,
In gratitude, we gently give.

So let us cherish every day,
In blossoming, we find our way.
With courage held and dreams to chase,
We start to bloom in life's embrace.

The Fire Within

In shadows deep, a spark ignites,
A whispered flame, illuminating nights.
With every breath, the heat expands,
Passion's dance within our hands.

Through trials faced, the embers glow,
Resilience found in heartbeats' flow.
Turning ashes to stories told,
A journey forged, brave and bold.

From fear to strength, the fire grows,
In every soul, the warmth bestows.
We rise above, refusing to wane,
The fire within, our fierce refrain.

So let it burn, this sacred light,
Guiding us through the darkest night.
Together we stand, hearts ablaze,
In the dance of the flames, we'll forever blaze.

Mirages of the Heart

Glimmers shimmer on the horizon,
Tender whispers, secrets risen.
In dreams we chase, an endless quest,
Mirages of love, we seek the best.

With petals soft, and shadows long,
A melody plays, an ancient song.
In twilight's embrace, visions appear,
A haunting beauty, both close and near.

Reflections bend in the desert's light,
Truth and illusion dance in flight.
In every heartbeat, a distant call,
To find the one who'll catch our fall.

With every sigh, the yearning grows,
Through paths of doubt, love gently flows.
In mirages clear, we find our place,
Bridging the distance, heart to grace.

Unveiling the Horizons

Beneath the stars, a canvas wide,
Dreams take flight, like waves that glide.
Horizons whisper of tales untold,
As dawn unveils its tapestry bold.

Colors merge in a symphony bright,
Every brushstroke ignites the night.
We stand as seekers, eyes open wide,
Embracing the journey, side by side.

The mountains loom, the oceans roar,
Each step we take, we crave for more.
In every moment, the world's embrace,
Unfolding wonders in time and space.

With courage like wings, we dare to soar,
Through valleys deep, to ocean's shore.
Unveiling horizons, we chase the sun,
A journey of hearts, forever spun.

Celestial Reflections

Stars above, like diamonds shine,
Mirrored thoughts that intertwine.
The universe speaks in silent ways,
In celestial reflections, we seek our days.

With moonlit dreams, we navigate,
In cosmic dances, we contemplate.
Each twinkle holds a story rare,
Connecting hearts with love and care.

Galaxies swirl, in vibrant dance,
In night's embrace, we find our chance.
Beneath the veil of endless skies,
Celestial whispers, where truth lies.

In stillness found, the soul takes flight,
As we become one with the night.
In this vast realm, our spirits blend,
Celestial reflections, our journey's mend.

Hidden Currents

Beneath the shimmering tide,
There are secrets that hide.
In caverns deep and dark,
Life's mysteries leave a mark.

Ripples of the past flow,
Whispering tales we know.
Through shadows and through light,
Hidden depths come to sight.

Currents twist and turn,
Lessons we shall learn.
With patience and grace,
We find our true place.

In the stillness, we see,
The dance of the sea.
As currents guide our way,
New paths start to play.

Embrace the unknown path,
Let go of the wrath.
In each hidden quirk,
Awaits a new spark.

Harmonies of the Heart

In whispers soft, the melodies rise,
Strings of desire weave through the skies.
Each note a promise, each chord a dream,
Hearts beat together, a rhythmic theme.

Under the moon, under starlit beams,
Love finds its way through fragile seams.
A symphony played in silence and light,
Binding us close, through day and night.

The dance of souls in a tender embrace,
Time stands still in this sacred space.
With every heartbeat, intentions align,
Together we rise, our spirits entwine.

In laughter and tears, we craft our song,
In joys and in sorrows, where we belong.
With harmonies rich, we paint the air,
A canvas of love, vibrant and rare.

As we sway to the music of fate,
In each other's presence, we resonate.
With every refrain, our hearts converge,
In the symphony of life, we gently purge.

Surrendering to the Silence

In the stillness, whispers retreat,
Echoes linger, where shadows meet.
Quiet moments, a breath away,
In surrender, we find our way.

The world fades softly into the night,
Thoughts drift gently, lost in flight.
A tranquil heart, a quiet mind,
In silence, the answers we find.

Beneath the stars, the vast unknown,
In the void, seeds of wisdom are sown.
With each heartbeat, we listen close,
To the soul's murmur, a whispered dose.

Letting go, we float in peace,
From the chaos, we find release.
In the tender hush, we come alive,
In the calm embrace, we thrive.

The canvas of silence paints the sky,
Where thoughts can wander, and spirits fly.
In the gentle light, we come to see,
Surrendering to silence, we simply be.

Navigating the Labyrinth

In twists and turns, my heart does roam,
Through winding paths, I seek my home.
Each corner hides a lesson vast,
In the maze of time, shadows are cast.

With every step, uncertainty grows,
Yet courage blooms where the wild wind blows.
Guided by stars that shine above,
I wander the paths, seeking love.

Mirrors reflect all I've overcome,
In the labyrinth's heart, I find my drum.
Rhythms of life play deep in me,
Echoing truths that set me free.

Though walls seem high and the way unclear,
I trust the journey, let go of fear.
In the tangle, I learn to strive,
Finding the strength to truly thrive.

Emerging from darkness, I greet the light,
The maze within becomes a guiding sight.
With every challenge, wisdom awaits,
In the labyrinth's weave, my soul elevates.

Guardians of the Subconscious

In shadows deep, the whispers weave,
Guardians dwell, in dreams they cleave.
Silent protectors of thoughts untold,
In the depths, their wisdom unfolds.

In the night, they unfurl their wings,
Cradling hopes, and lost offerings.
With gentle hands, they guide our way,
Through ancient paths where shadows play.

Echoes of secrets, soft and low,
In the silence, they help us grow.
From fears released, to courage found,
Guardians linger, all around.

Through tangled webs of the heart and mind,
Enlightenment waits, patiently aligned.
In the realms unseen, their grace is vast,
Holding the keys to futures cast.

So when you dream, take heed and trust,
For in the dark, they rise from dust.
Guardians watch with love profound,
In the subconscious, our truths are found.

Echoes of Self

In the silence, whispers unfold,
Secrets of the heart, untold.
Mirror images dance in light,
Shadows linger, soft as night.

Through the halls of thought I roam,
Chasing dreams that feel like home.
A symphony of voices blend,
In solitude, we find our mend.

Fleeting moments, time's embrace,
Each heartbeat, a sacred space.
Reflections call from deep within,
A journey traced on paper skin.

Echoes linger, soft and true,
Guiding paths where once I flew.
In every dawn, new shades reveal,
The tender pulse of what I feel.

A tapestry of vibrant hues,
In every choice, the self renews.
Through the echoes, I will soar,
Embracing what I was before.

Beneath the Surface

Ripples dance on water's edge,
Secrets whispered, make a pledge.
Beneath the calm, a world awakes,
Where silence stirs, and stillness quakes.

Hints of color, deep and bright,
Lurking shadows, out of sight.
Waves of thought, they ebb and flow,
Heartfelt currents, deep below.

In the depths, a longing grew,
Yearning souls, forever true.
Diving deeper, I will find,
The hidden treasures left behind.

Conversations with the unknown,
Beneath the surface, seeds are sown.
In every sigh and tender sigh,
A world awaits to amplify.

As the ocean swells and dips,
Emotions rise on gentle lips.
Beneath the waves, the truth remains,
A subtle dance, where love sustains.

Awakening the Heart's Compass

In quiet moments, stars align,
Guiding souls, a thread divine.
Awakening the heart's embrace,
A compass found, a sacred space.

Through forests deep, my spirit roams,
Mapping paths to hidden homes.
With every step, the rhythm shares,
The pulse of life; the heart declares.

Winds of change, they whisper clear,
A journey starts as dreams draw near.
In every heartbeat, lessons weave,
A tapestry of hopes believe.

The journey's call, a gentle nudge,
To rise above and feel the surge.
Embracing fate with open hands,
The compass points to promised lands.

Awakening the truth inside,
A map of love where dreams abide.
With every breath, I'll navigate,
The boundaries blur; I learn to wait.

Reflections of a Hidden Flame

Beneath the surface, embers glow,
Secrets held that few may know.
In quiet corners, passions rise,
Reflections dance in muffled sighs.

The heart ignites with fleeting spark,
Illuminating paths through dark.
In shadows deep, desires sway,
Awakening the night to day.

Moments flicker, soft and bright,
Weaving warmth into the night.
A flame that whispers, soft and low,
A guiding light, in whispers flow.

From ashes rise a new refrain,
In quietude, we break the chain.
A reflection formed in tender grace,
The hidden flame finds its place.

With every flicker, I will dance,
Embracing fate, extending chance.
In heart and soul, the fire remains,
A testament to love's refrains.

Threads of Consciousness

In the fabric of our minds,
Threads of thoughts entwine,
Weaving dreams and fears,
A dance through space and time.

Whispers echo in the night,
Stories left untold,
Fleeting shadows of our truth,
In the silence, we behold.

Colors blend, a vivid hue,
Moments caught in grace,
Frayed edges of our memories,
In this delicate embrace.

Awake to dawn's soft light,
The tapestry unfolds,
Each strand a tale of longing,
A journey brave and bold.

In this intricate design,
We search for our own thread,
To stitch together pieces,
Of the life we want to lead.

Constellations of the Self

In the night, stars gently gleam,
Mapping paths of forgotten dreams.
Whispers of light call, softly bright,
Guardians of truth in the endless night.

Each pulse of life, a cosmic dance,
Echoes of time in fleeting glance.
Journeys weave through dark and light,
In constellations of self, we ignite.

Fragments of starlight fill the void,
In silent spaces, souls are buoyed.
Threads of fate connect us all,
Through constellations, we rise and fall.

Mirrors reflecting the vast unknown,
In every sigh, a universe grown.
Embrace the pattern of your own star,
And find your place, no matter how far.

Trust in the cosmos, it knows your name,
Guiding the heart through joy and pain.
In the tapestry of night, be bold,
For you are a story yet to be told.

Tides of Transformation

Waves crash upon the shore,
Changing sands once more.
Every swell tells a tale,
Of journeys brave and frail.

With each rising sun,
New beginnings have begun.
The moon pulls the sea,
Dancing wild and free.

In the depths of change,
Life may feel strange.
Yet, beneath the foam,
We carve a new home.

Echoes of old dreams,
Flow like gentle streams.
As tides shift and roam,
We craft our own dome.

As the world spins round,
New strengths shall be found.
In the ebb and flow,
We learn to let go.

Reverberations of the Heart

Echoes linger in the quiet air,
Whispers of longing, secrets laid bare.
Each beat a story, each sigh a song,
In reverberations, we all belong.

Moments captured in tender glance,
Fleeting touches, a timeless dance.
Hearts in rhythm, a pulsing beat,
In the silence, we find our heat.

Words unspoken drift like clouds,
Carrying dreams in gentle shrouds.
Emotions rise, a rising tide,
In the waves, we cannot hide.

Love's sweet call, a siren's tune,
Guiding hearts beneath the moon.
In harmony's grasp, we intertwine,
Through reverberations, your heart is mine.

Together, we mold the fragile sound,
In the heart's resonance, we are bound.
An echo of hope that will not part,
Forever alive in the reverberant heart.

Embracing the Unfamiliar

Step into shadows, where silence breathes,
In depths unknown, adventure weaves.
New roads beckon, fear slips away,
In embracing unknown, we find our way.

Colors burst in unexpected light,
Transform the dark into vibrant sight.
Each twist and turn, a chance to grow,
In unfamiliar paths, courage flows.

Voices call from beyond our shell,
Stories untold that bid us to dwell.
With open hearts, let the journey start,
Every stranger may play a part.

Discovering beauty in the unknown,
In unlikely places, seeds are sown.
Embrace the risks, let go of the plan,
In the unfamiliar, you'll find who you am.

Life is a canvas, vast and wide,
Filled with hues of the unknown tide.
In every encounter, a lesson awaits,
Embrace the journey that destiny creates.

Unfurling Inner Petals

In the stillness, whispers arise,
Petals unfold, as the spirit tries.
Layers reveal what's deep inside,
In the garden of self, take pride.

Gentle breezes coax them to bloom,
In sunlight's grace, they dispel gloom.
Each color vibrant, each scent a prayer,
Unfurling petals, a soul laid bare.

Time is the water, patience the sun,
In nurturing silence, we all become.
With each unfolding, strength is found,
In life's great cycle, we are unbound.

Embrace the journey of self-discovery,
In every petal, find your recovery.
Let the inner garden flourish and thrive,
Through unfurling petals, we feel alive.

At the heart of growth, there lies a spark,
Illuminate the shadows, chase the dark.
In the bloom of the self, love will reside,
As we unfurl inner petals with pride.

Navigating the Silent Waters

Beneath a tranquil sky so vast,
Silent waters gently flow,
In the stillness, reflections gleam,
Of the paths we do not know.

Ripples formed by whispered dreams,
Guide us through the haze,
In each wave, a story waits,
In the silence, hearts ablaze.

Stars above, a map of hope,
To steer our drifting souls,
In quiet moments, courage births,
As the journey softly rolls.

With every stroke, we chart our course,
Amongst the calm and storm,
Navigating deep emotions,
Where true selves transform.

Each journey whispers secrets,
In the waters' gentle sway,
Finding strength in solitude,
As the night gives way to day.

Seeds of Self-Discovery

In the garden of the soul,
Seeds of thought are sown,
With care and gentle hands,
Dreams begin to bloom.

Nurtured by the light within,
They stretch toward the sun,
Filling the air with promise,
And wonders yet begun.

Roots run deep in fertile ground,
Anchored by the past,
Each petal tells a story,
Of moments meant to last.

With every tear and laughter shared,
A blossom finds its place,
In the vastness of the heart,
Each flower holds a trace.

As seasons change and time moves on,
We cultivate and grow,
In the soil of our being,
The truth begins to show.

Uncharted Horizons

Beneath a sky of endless blue,
We chase the dreams we want to find.
With every step, a journey new,
A world awaits, the bold unwind.

Mountains rise where shadows dwell,
Rivers flow with tales untold.
Through whispering winds, the secrets swell,
A path untraveled, brave and bold.

Stars ignite the night's embrace,
While dawn awakens hope anew.
Adventure calls, we'll find our place,
In realms where skies hold endless view.

The horizon beckons, drawing near,
With open hearts, we greet the day.
As we explore, we shed our fear,
In uncharted lands, we choose to stay.

Together, hand in hand we tread,
In every step, a story thrives.
With courage sewn, our spirits fed,
We paint our fate as dreamers' lives.

Dance of the Hidden Heart

In shadows where the silence sings,
The heart awakens, beats anew.
A dance entwined with whispered things,
With every step, we're drawn right through.

Fingers brush on fleeting dreams,
A spark ignites, the passion flows.
In secret glances, sunlight beams,
The dance of love, the heartbeat knows.

In crowded rooms, we find the space,
Where rhythms pulse and souls align.
A hidden dance, a sweet embrace,
In every spin, our fates combine.

The melody of life composed,
In notes of joy and soft despair.
In every twirl, our truth exposed,
As hearts collide, we boldly dare.

In twilight's glow, we lose all fear,
For love's the dance we long to start.
In each beat, it grows more clear,
Together, we are one heart's art.

Flames of Transformation

From ashes, rise, the phoenix glows,
In fiery hues, we shed our skin.
Each flicker holds the strength one knows,
In flames of change, new lives begin.

The blaze ignites with every tear,
Transforming pain to polished light.
In burning truth, we conquer fear,
From darkness comes the dawn so bright.

Embers whisper of what's to gain,
As we embrace the heat inside.
With every shift, we break the chain,
In flames of hope, our dreams collide.

The fire dances, wild and free,
Consuming doubt, igniting grace.
In courage found, we come to be,
As flames of passion change our pace.

We rise anew, reborn and whole,
In every flicker, truth is sown.
Through fire's gift, we claim our role,
And in that heat, our strength is grown.

Guardians of the Inner Realm

In sacred spaces, stillness reigns,
Where echoes weave through time and dreams.
Guardians stand, holding the reins,
In silence, hear the universe's schemes.

With whispered vows, we seek to know,
The truths that dwell beneath the skin.
In realms unseen, the light will show,
The paths to take, where love begins.

Each heartbeat guides the way we tread,
Through shadows cast by doubt and fear.
With wisdom brewed, it's gently said,
In stillness, every truth is clear.

The spirits dance in twilight's glow,
Guardians of dreams, we claim our space.
In heart's embrace, we freely flow,
For in this realm, we find our grace.

The inner realm, a sacred place,
Where whispers turn to whispered art.
As guardians rise with gentle face,
We journey deep, one soul, one heart.

Canvas of the Mind

Upon the canvas, colors blend,
Dreams and thoughts, a spectrum lend.
Each stroke a whisper, soft and bright,
Crafting visions born from light.

Shadows mingle with the hue,
Stories whispered, old and new.
Fragments of memory take their form,
In the heart, a quiet storm.

Brushes dance with gentle grace,
Capturing time, each fleeting space.
Moments held in vibrant thread,
A tapestry of life widespread.

Layers deep, emotions flow,
In every corner, stories grow.
The mind's a gallery, vast and wide,
With paintings where our truths reside.

So let the colors never cease,
In this world, find your peace.
With every hue, a story told,
In the canvas of the bold.

A Tapestry of Thoughts

In the loom of quiet minds,
Threads of thought unite,
Patterns form in colors bright,
As day surrenders night.

Woven moments intertwine,
In every breath and sigh,
Ideas dance like fireflies,
Beneath the velvet sky.

Each stitch a tale of dreams,
Fragile yet so bold,
Stories rich as ancient myths,
In our hearts they're told.

Knots of worry, threads of hope,
The fabric shifts with grace,
A tapestry of memories,
In our shared embrace.

As the world spins in a blur,
We find our rhythm's beat,
In the woven strands of life,
Where love and wisdom meet.

Threads of Consciousness

Weaving thoughts like threads of gold,
Stories waiting to be told.
In whispers soft, they intertwine,
A tapestry of the divine.

Each thread a moment, bright or dim,
With echoes of what might have been.
In the loom of life, we stand,
Crafting futures with our hand.

Connections spark with gentle grace,
Bringing warmth to every space.
Across the fabric, visions flow,
As the heart learns what to sow.

Through pain and joy, the threads align,
A dance of fate, a sacred sign.
In every twist, a purpose finds,
The ultimate, the boundless kinds.

Together we create and mend,
An endless loop without an end.
In unity, our truths are found,
In these threads, we're tightly bound.

In Search of Wholeness

In shadows long and echoes deep,
We yearn for truths we strive to keep.
Scattered pieces of our soul,
Seeking balance, seeking whole.

Through rivers wide and mountains tall,
We wander, answering the call.
The whispers of the heart guide on,
Through twilight's glow to the dawn.

Fragments glimmer in the light,
Each one holds a spark of fight.
In the mosaic of our scars,
We find a map of where we are.

With every step, the journey flows,
In seeking wisdom, the spirit grows.
The path may twist, the road may bend,
But in each heart, the search won't end.

So gather pieces, near and far,
In the darkness, be your star.
With love and grace, we will find,
The wholeness wrapped in heart and mind.

Gentle Unraveling

In quiet moments, threads unwind,
Revealing truths, with peace aligned.
A soft embrace, the heart lets go,
In stillness, deeper currents flow.

The fabric of our days revealed,
In each surrender, love is healed.
As layers peel, the spirit breathes,
In gentle storms, the heart believes.

Each unraveling, a sacred act,
Finding beauty in what is cracked.
For in the flaws, the light shines through,
A tapestry of me and you.

With open hands, we shift and bend,
Letting love once more transcend.
In letting go, we learn to see,
The endless depths of what can be.

So let us weave with threads of grace,
In this dance, find our true place.
In gentle unraveling, we find the way,
To embrace each fleeting day.

The Pulse of the Universe

Stars whisper softly in the night,
Galaxies dance in fleeting light.
Each heartbeat echoes through the vast,
Moments captured, shadows cast.

Infinity spins in cosmic grace,
Time unfolds in endless space.
Celestial rhythms guide the way,
Lost in dreams where silence sways.

Light years travel in a single breath,
Eternal stories weave through death.
Constellations map the soul's intent,
In the hush, our dreams are lent.

Waves of stardust gently flow,
In this mystic dance, we grow.
With every pulse, the universe sings,
Carrying hope on cosmic wings.

As we listen to the cosmic breeze,
In our hearts, we find the keys.
Unlock the secrets, take your flight,
Embrace the void, ignite the night.

Sacred Space of Being

In the stillness, where shadows play,
Silent whispers guide the way.
Between each breath, a world unfolds,
In sacred space, the truth beholds.

Time suspends in gentle grace,
Every moment, a holy place.
Feel the pulse of life within,
In this sanctuary, we begin.

Wisdom blooms in quiet thoughts,
In the silence, peace is sought.
With open hearts, we come alive,
In sacred space, we learn to thrive.

Fragments of light, glimmers of hope,
In this embrace, we learn to cope.
Every heartbeat, a love song sings,
In sacred space, the spirit springs.

A tapestry stitched with dreams and care,
In this haven, we understand where.
Journey onward, let spirits soar,
In sacred space, forevermore.

The Heart's Compass

In the quiet, the heart does speak,
Guiding paths for those who seek.
With every rhythm, wisdom flows,
  Navigating where love grows.

Through valleys deep and mountains high,
  The compass whispers, never shy.
  Trust the journey, follow the call,
  Embrace the rise, accept the fall.

With courage blazing like the sun,
Every heartbeat, we become one.
Mapping dreams on uncharted seas,
  In the embrace of gentle breeze.

In the laughter and the tears,
In every moment, conquer fears.
The heart's compass, a steadfast guide,
  In its embrace, joy will abide.

With intuition as our map,
We journey forth, escape the trap.
Let feelings lead, let spirit flow,
In the heart's compass, love will grow.

Secrets of the Inner Wind

Whispers carried by the breeze,
Voice of nature, soft with ease.
Through the trees, a song is spun,
Secrets linger, hidden, undone.

In the rustle, stories weave,
Echoes of the hearts that grieve.
In every gust, a lesson found,
Gentle nudges, life unbound.

Feel the currents, let them guide,
In the flow, let worries subside.
The inner wind knows where to roam,
In its embrace, we find our home.

Listen closely to the sighs,
In the silence, wisdom lies.
With each breath, the secrets spin,
In the dance of the inner wind.

Let the whispers shape your song,
In their arms, you will belong.
Transforming doubt into pure grace,
Secrets flourish in this space.

The Music of the Unseen

Whispers dance upon the air,
In shadows, notes begin to flare.
The silence carries hidden tunes,
While starlight hums to silver moons.

Echoes woven through the night,
Invisible, yet full of light.
Each heartbeat plays a subtle part,
A symphony of the human heart.

Beneath the surface, rhythms swell,
In every soul, a story dwells.
The music flows, both soft and grand,
A harmony we understand.

In twilight's grasp, the notes do soar,
Through silence, like a gentle roar.
A serenade of shadows spins,
A tapestry where life begins.

Feel the pulse in every sound,
Where unseen melodies abound.
The world ignites as whispers cling,
A bond of life, the songbirds sing.

Illumination of the Mind

Thoughts flicker like candlelight,
In the corners of the night.
Ideas blossom, bright and bold,
In shadows where the dreams unfold.

Wisdom dances in the dark,
A spark ignites, igniting stark.
Words become a guiding star,
Leading us to lands afar.

The mind's horizon stretches wide,
With every thought, a thrilling ride.
Imagination blooms like dawn,
In the silence, new worlds are born.

Reality bends, time unwinds,
In the light, our purpose finds.
Illumination warms the soul,
As knowledge makes the spirit whole.

We seek the truth in every line,
A journey through the vast divine.
In the mind's expanse, we roam,
Finding the light that leads us home.

Solar Flare of the Spirit

Radiance spills from inner glow,
A fiery pulse begins to flow.
In the heart, a sun ignites,
Illuminating darkest nights.

Energies twist and brightly shine,
In vibrant hues, our spirits entwine.
A burst of light, a wave of heat,
In every challenge, we find our beat.

Cosmic winds lift dreams on high,
As we reach for the endless sky.
An aura born from depths within,
A solar flare, where greatness begins.

With every breath, we share the flame,
An essence wild, we cannot tame.
The spirit dances, fierce and free,
A testament of who we can be.

Embrace the warmth, let it inspire,
Our passions blaze with fierce desire.
United, we will shine so bright,
In the solar flare of pure delight.

Gardens of Tranquility

In silence where the lilies grow,
Gentle whispers ebb and flow.
A sanctuary, calm and deep,
Where weary souls can find their sleep.

Petals soft as twilight's breath,
In every corner, life and death.
Harmony within each bloom,
A sacred space, a quiet room.

The rustle of the leaves, a song,
In the stillness where we belong.
Moments pause to feel the breeze,
Among the trees, find sweet release.

Colors blend in soothing hues,
To evoke the soul's deep muse.
Here in this garden of delight,
Our hearts can dance in purest light.

From fragrant earth, new hopes arise,
As dreams take root beneath our skies.
In the tranquility we find,
A space of peace, a gentle mind.

Dreams Beneath the Surface

In twilight's soft embrace, we roam,
Where whispers of the night call home.
Beneath the waves, secrets lie,
In the cradle of the sky.

Echoes dance on silver streams,
Carrying our faded dreams.
With each ripple, hopes arise,
Like constellations in our eyes.

Shadows merge with twilight's grace,
As we search for our place.
In the depth, our spirits twine,
Lost in a world that's divine.

Echoing the heart's desires,
Fanning softly hidden fires.
With every breath, the surface breaks,
As we wear our heart in flakes.

Beneath the sky, we find our part,
Chasing dreams that fill the heart.
In the waters, clarity lies,
Our reflections in the sighs.

Reflections in the Deep

Beneath the waves, a world unfolds,
Where dreams are caught in tales retold.
Mirrors whispering secrets bright,
In shadows dancing, out of sight.

Glimmers of truth beneath the foam,
Invite us to make the depths our home.
Each surge carries a piece of fate,
In this realm where time stands straight.

Ripples hold a silent song,
Echoing stories, fierce and strong.
In the still, the chaos thaws,
Revealing nature's hidden laws.

Deep within, our hearts entwine,
In the silence, love divine.
Reflections spin in liquid grace,
Capturing dreams we dare to trace.

As the tides gently shift and sway,
We discover light in shadows' play.
In the deep, we find our voice,
In the whispers, we rejoice.

Embracing the Void

In the stillness, silence reigns,
Whispers echo through the pains.
The void offers a calm embrace,
Where fears dissolve without a trace.

Here, in shadows, light does weave,
Threads of hope we dare believe.
In absence, we find strength anew,
As darkness dances, true and blue.

With every heartbeat, courage grows,
In the hollow, potential flows.
The void teaches what it means,
To find our light in unseen scenes.

We sail through nights painted in gray,
Finding comfort in the sway.
In the emptiness, we ignite,
A universe within our sight.

Embracing all that life can give,
In the void, we learn to live.
Together bound, our spirits soar,
In the stillness, we are more.

Radiant Mirrors

In twilight's glow, reflections shine,
We see ourselves in each design.
Each radiant mirror holds a tale,
Of dreams we seek and paths we trail.

Glancing back at what we've known,
In every shard, our essence shown.
Mirrors glimmer with every breath,
Whispers of life, beyond mere death.

Through the glass, we catch a spark,
Illuminating the hidden dark.
What once was lost now finds its place,
In every fragment, a warm embrace.

In radiant colors, stories blend,
Creating bridges that transcend.
Together, we reflect the light,
In every moment, bold and bright.

So let us dance in hues of gold,
Embrace the stories yet untold.
In radiant mirrors, we unite,
Living dreams, taking flight.

Whispers of the Soul

In the stillness of the night,
Dreams take flight, soft and bright.
Echoes wrap around the heart,
Whispers speak, never to part.

Secrets hidden in the mist,
Gentle sighs, moments missed.
Through the shadows, voices call,
Guiding weary souls through all.

Stars above shimmer and gleam,
In their glow, we find our dream.
Every heartbeat, every breath,
A dance of life that conquers death.

Memories weave like silver thread,
In the tapestry, words unsaid.
Hope ignites with every dawn,
A promise kept, a love reborn.

With every whisper, spirits rise,
Unseen bonds connect the skies.
In the silence, we confide,
Together still, side by side.

Whispers of the Soul

In the stillness of the night,
Dreams take flight, soft and bright.
Echoes wrap around the heart,
Whispers speak, never to part.

Secrets hidden in the mist,
Gentle sighs, moments missed.
Through the shadows, voices call,
Guiding weary souls through all.

Stars above shimmer and gleam,
In their glow, we find our dream.
Every heartbeat, every breath,
A dance of life that conquers death.

Memories weave like silver thread,
In the tapestry, words unsaid.
Hope ignites with every dawn,
A promise kept, a love reborn.

With every whisper, spirits rise,
Unseen bonds connect the skies.
In the silence, we confide,
Together still, side by side.

Radiant Mirrors

In twilight's glow, reflections shine,
We see ourselves in each design.
Each radiant mirror holds a tale,
Of dreams we seek and paths we trail.

Glancing back at what we've known,
In every shard, our essence shown.
Mirrors glimmer with every breath,
Whispers of life, beyond mere death.

Through the glass, we catch a spark,
Illuminating the hidden dark.
What once was lost now finds its place,
In every fragment, a warm embrace.

In radiant colors, stories blend,
Creating bridges that transcend.
Together, we reflect the light,
In every moment, bold and bright.

So let us dance in hues of gold,
Embrace the stories yet untold.
In radiant mirrors, we unite,
Living dreams, taking flight.

When Shadows Dance

Beneath the moon's soft glow,
Whispers rise, shadows flow.
Footsteps echo in the night,
Where the dark meets the light.

Figures swirl in mystic grace,
Veils of night, they interlace.
Crickets sing their lullabies,
As the world begins to rise.

Every rustle carries tales,
Of forgotten paths and trails.
In the silence, hearts collide,
Where the shadows twist and bide.

Time stands still in this embrace,
Moments captured in their place.
When the stars align just right,
Magic dances through the night.

With each heartbeat, shadows sway,
Guiding dreams that drift away.
In the twilight, spirits prance,
Lost in the rhythm, when shadows dance.

Beneath the Silent Veil

Veils of whispers softly call,
Secrets hanging, poised to fall.
In the depth of quiet skies,
Awaiting truth that never lies.

Gentle winds weave through the trees,
Carrying echoes on the breeze.
Moments linger, time stands still,
In the hush, we seek the thrill.

Underneath the starry dome,
Souls connect, we find our home.
Infinite stories intertwine,
In the shadows, hearts align.

Every silence tells a tale,
Of a journey, bright or pale.
In the calm, we gather light,
Beneath the veil, dark turns bright.

With each thought, we paint the air,
Colors merging, bold and fair.
In the quiet, we can hear,
A symphony that draws us near.

Echoes of Forgotten Light

In the hallways of the mind,
Memories twist and unwind.
Flickers of what used to be,
Echoes whisper, setting free.

Through the fog of time we tread,
Carrying stories long since dead.
In the twilight's tender grace,
We find solace in this space.

Faint reflections flicker bright,
Remnants of forgotten light.
Each glimmer a fleeting flame,
Calling forth an ancient name.

In the shadow's soft embrace,
Dreams resurface, time can trace.
As we wander through the years,
Finding joy, confronting fears.

With each echo, life will grow,
Planting seeds of hope to sow.
In the stillness, we will find,
That love's voice shall not be blind.

Unveiling the Inner Muse

In silence whispers soft and clear,
A spark ignites, the path draws near.
Thoughts entwined, like vines they climb,
Awakening dreams, transcending time.

With colors bright, the canvas waits,
A dance of shadows, opening gates.
Brush and vision, hand in hand,
Unfolding tales across the land.

Echoes linger, stories unsung,
A symphony of soul begun.
In every heartbeat, truths reside,
With every breath, the muse must guide.

Through tangled paths, I learn to see,
The hidden heart that longs to be.
Whispers grow to shouts of grace,
As I unveil the sacred space.

In gentle flow, the verses blend,
Embracing love that knows no end.
Awake my spirit, rise and soar,
With every verse, I am reborn.

Dreams Beneath the Veil

In twilight's grasp, the silent sighs,
Where hidden dreams in shadows lie.
They twirl and weave like threads of night,
Yearning for dawn, to chase the light.

Beneath the veil, the whispers hum,
Stories waiting to be spun.
In secret gardens, visions bloom,
Awakening the heart from gloom.

Each fragile hope, a star so bright,
Guiding souls through endless night.
With every heartbeat, hope ignites,
Chasing shadows, claiming heights.

In depths of silence, treasures sleep,
Promises made, forever keep.
The veil shall lift, as dreams take flight,
Transcending dark, embracing light.

Awoken now, the spirits sing,
Of dreams and hopes, they gently bring.
Together we break through the shell,
And dance in joy, all is well.

Rising from Within

From ashes cold, a fire grows,
With flickers bright, the spirit shows.
In depths of night, a voice ascends,
With every breath, the journey bends.

Awakening strength from silent depths,
A rising tide, it gently sweeps.
Roots intertwined, we stand as one,
Emerging strong, a new day's sun.

In stillness found, the heart beats loud,
Echoes roaring, fierce and proud.
Courage blooms where fear once dwelled,
And stories told of how we felled.

Embrace the light, let shadows fade,
With every step, foundations laid.
In unity, our voices blend,
A rising force that shall not bend.

The dawn unfolds with colors rare,
A tapestry of dreams and care.
Together we rise, bold and free,
Illuminated, our true decree.

Illuminating the Shadows

In dim-lit corners, secrets stir,
A gentle glow, a whispered word.
From darkened paths, the light emerges,
As shadows bow and fear diverges.

With every flicker, doubts take flight,
Illuminated by soft insight.
The dance of light, a tender spell,
Revealing truths we long to tell.

In hidden places, courage blooms,
Chasing away the shadowed fumes.
Together we stand, hand in hand,
Unveiling light across the land.

The heart's desire sheds heavy chains,
As wisdom flows through gentle rains.
Each step forward, a spark ignites,
Illuminating darkest nights.

With every heartbeat, shadows flee,
As light expands, we come to be.
Together we shine through pain and strife,
Illuminating all of life.

A Symphony of Self

In the quiet dawn, I find my tune,
Notes of passion under the moon.
A melody built of dreams and fears,
Harmonizing whispers through the years.

Each chord is woven from my soul,
Echoes of laughter, a story whole.
Resonance in every breath I take,
Crafting a rhythm that will not break.

Through crescendos of joy, I soar high,
Soft ballads of sorrow make me cry.
This symphony plays, both fierce and tender,
An opus of life, my heart's defender.

The strings of hope vibrate within,
As I dance on the edge of the din.
Bringing together each part of me,
Creating music that sets me free.

In every silence, a note remains,
In every heartbeat, the music reigns.
I join the chorus, a vibrant voice,
In this grand symphony, I rejoice.

The Alchemy of Being

Elements of earth in restless play,
Transforming shadows into light of day.
A spark ignites in the depths of soul,
Turning the mundane into the whole.

Through fire and water, I find my way,
Shaping my spirit, come what may.
With every challenge, I learn to bend,
Crafting solutions that never end.

Gold of wisdom formed from grief,
The weight of sorrow, a hidden relief.
I mix memories, both bitter and sweet,
In this cauldron of life, I feel the heat.

A potion brewed from the heart's embrace,
Finding my magic in every space.
I rise like vapor, a luminous stream,
In the alchemy of being, I dream.

This metamorphosis flares bold and bright,
Illuminating passages of night.
With each rebirth, my essence unfurls,
Transforming the fabric of hidden worlds.

Lost and Found

In the labyrinth of thought I roam,
Searching for fragments that once felt like home.
Shadows whisper secrets to my heart,
Guiding me gently back to the start.

Memories flicker like candles in dark,
Each flame a reminder, a flickering spark.
Moments forgotten, like leaves on the ground,
Yet in their rustle, my truth can be found.

Through the maze of sorrow, I stumble and tread,
Unearthing treasures in words left unsaid.
Embracing the losses that shape who I am,
In the depths of despair, I learn to stand.

The echoes of laughter dance on the breeze,
Promises made are much more than mere pleas.
In the tapestry woven with threads of the past,
I gather my pieces, my heart beats steadfast.

In finding what's lost, I discover anew,
A strength in the journey, profound and true.
With open arms, I welcome the grace,
Of both the lost and the found in this space.

The Pulse of Potential

In the stillness of dawn, a heartbeat stirs,
Awakening dreams where potential blurs.
Each pulse a whisper, a promise of light,
Guiding the way through the cover of night.

A current flows, bursting forth in fire,
Daring the limits, igniting desire.
With every rhythm, I rise to ignite,
The spark of creation, a dazzling flight.

From shadows to brilliance, I reach, I climb,
Lifting my spirit, transcending time.
Each beat a stepping stone to the sky,
Unfolding the wings of the daring fly.

A symphony dances in endless array,
Urging me forward, come what may.
In the pulse of potential, I find my way,
Crafting my world, day after day.

In the depths of my being, it whispers 'believe,'
The promise of greatness, it's mine to achieve.
As the pulse resonates, I start to ascend,
A journey of growth with no end.

Refuges of the Mind

In quiet corners, thoughts reside,
Where whispers echo, dreams confide.
A sanctuary, soft and bright,
In shadows deep, they find their light.

Time slows down within these walls,
A gentle voice, as silence calls.
Worries fade, like morning dew,
In this haven, all feels new.

With every breath, a peace unfolds,
A tapestry of stories told.
Here, the heart can safely roam,
And weave its path in threads of home.

Thoughts like rivers softly flow,
In this refuge, let them grow.
To know oneself, a sacred quest,
In the stillness, spirits rest.

Embrace the whispers, let them guide,
On this journey, walk with pride.
For in the mind's vast, tender space,
We find our truths, our rightful place.

Shifting Sands of Identity

Beneath the surface, layers shift,
A mosaic formed from every gift.
Each tide that pulls, each wave that breaks,
Transforms the shore, and yet, it wakes.

Mirrors crack, yet still reflect,
The fragments here we can connect.
In every change, a part must go,
To let the new and vibrant grow.

Roots dig deep in shifting ground,
Yet scattered seeds still seek the sound.
Of voices, old and yet so new,
A chorus formed, a vibrant hue.

As seasons turn, we take our shape,
From firm resolve to soft escape.
Identity, a dance we learn,
In constant flux, we twist and turn.

With every step, a story grows,
In shifting sands where wisdom flows.
Embrace the change, let go of fear,
For every phase, the self is near.

A journey vast, yet all our own,
Through trials faced, we have been shown.
From every grain, our truth we find,
In the endless sands of the mind.

Sparks of Insight

A flicker in the darkened night,
A sudden flash, a guiding light.
Ideas dance like fireflies,
Illuminating hidden ties.

In quiet moments, thoughts collide,
A spark ignites, and worlds collide.
Potential brews in silent seas,
As wisdom whispers in the breeze.

With each discovery, we ignite,
Passion burning, fierce and bright.
From ember small to roaring flame,
The heart awakens, knowing its name.

Threads of insight weave through time,
In rhythmic flow, a gentle rhyme.
Embrace the sparks that come alive,
In open minds, they thrive and strive.

In every challenge, light appears,
Through doubts and fears, the path clears.
An inner voice begins to sing,
Of truths unearthed and hope to bring.

So gather 'round, let thoughts ignite,
With every spark, we share our light.
Together, we will shape the way,
As insights bloom and dreams convey.

Veils of Awareness

In layers soft, we find our truth,
Beneath the noise, the whispers soothe.
With gentle hands, we peel away,
The veils that hide the light of day.

Each veil a story, old and worn,
In shadows deep, we're often torn.
Yet clarity shines through the mist,
Awareness grows, we must persist.

Awake, unmask the hidden fears,
In stillness, let them disappear.
For in the light, all things shall blend,
As we uncover and amend.

With every breath, the layers fall,
Revealing essence to us all.
A tapestry of truths untold,
In vibrant threads, life's hues unfold.

The path to self, a winding road,
Through veils of time, we bear our load.
Yet, stripped of doubt, we stand so clear,
In insights deep, we find our sphere.

So let the veils drift softly down,
And wear our truths like a crown.
In awareness found, we learn to see,
The beauty of our legacy.

Unfolding Awareness

In the dawn, a whisper calls,
Soft light breaks through the walls.
Every thought begins to bloom,
Awareness spreads like sweet perfume.

Fractured dreams start to align,
In this moment, I confine.
The universe sings its song,
A sacred space where I belong.

Eyes wide open, I engage,
Turning every single page.
Life's mysteries, I embrace,
In stillness, I find my place.

With each breath, I rise anew,
Finding strength in what's true.
Thoughts like rivers, flowing free,
In this truth, I find my key.

Awareness unfolds, a gentle tide,
Carrying me to the inside.
In each moment, I can see,
This unfolding is the real me.

Threads of Existence

In the fabric of the night,
Threads of stars begin to light.
Woven stories, old and new,
Binding all, in endless view.

Life's tapestry so vast,
Moments interlaced and cast.
Every heart beats in the glow,
Feel the pulse of all we know.

Soft connections, unseen ties,
Whispered truths, beneath the skies.
Every person plays their part,
Stitching dreams with open heart.

In the silence, echoes play,
Threads of laughter guide the way.
Through the weave, we find our sound,
In this dance, we are unbound.

United in this grand design,
Every thread, a life aligned.
In the loom, our spirits soar,
Threads of existence, forevermore.

In the Stillness of Being

In the hush of endless time,
Where thoughts dissolve like fading rhyme.
Moments pause, the world is near,
In the stillness, I feel clear.

Silent whispers fill the air,
Each breath taken, a gentle prayer.
Echoes of the heart resound,
In this calm, peace is found.

Thoughts like clouds drift far away,
Leaving space for light to play.
In the quiet, I am free,
In the stillness, I can see.

Time flows softly, like a stream,
Carrying the weight of dream.
In this moment, I belong,
A melody, a soothing song.

Being rests in quiet grace,
In this stillness, I embrace.
Every heartbeat, every sigh,
In the stillness, I can fly.

Elysium of Thoughts

In a realm where dreams reside,
Thoughts like blossoms open wide.
Each idea a vibrant hue,
In this garden, I renew.

Golden rays filter through leaves,
Touching what my spirit weaves.
Imagination takes its flight,
Painting days with pure delight.

In this sanctuary of mind,
Every pathway intertwined.
Whispers linger on the breeze,
Inviting hearts to find their ease.

Every spark, a brand new start,
Elysium lives within the heart.
Through the chaos, I will tread,
Finding wisdom, softly spread.

Thoughts like rivers, vast and free,
Flowing through infinity.
In this space, I come alive,
In the Elysium, I thrive.

Labyrinth of the Soul

In shadows deep, the dreams reside,
A winding path, where fears abide.
Each corner turned, a silent call,
    Echoes whisper in the hall.

The heart, a maze, with walls of dread,
Where thoughts are tangled, softly spread.
A light that flickers, faint yet bold,
    Guides the seeker, truth untold.

Labyrinthine, the soul's design,
Threaded through with moments divine.
Finding peace in every twist,
    Each step a chance not to resist.

Yet courage blooms in darkest night,
    Illuminating hidden sight.
For in this dance, the heart can learn,
    That every page awaits a turn.

To wander deep, to lose and find,
In silent chambers, hopes unwind.
For every path that veers away,
Leads to the dawn of a new day.

The Echo of Existence

In the stillness, voices rise,
Whispers soft as starlit skies.
Each breath a note, a fleeting sound,
Life's melody, profound, unbound.

Mountains tall and rivers wide,
Breathe together, side by side.
Nature hums a timeless tune,
Underneath the watchful moon.

As shadows dance and sunlight plays,
Life's grand saga weaves and stays.
An echo calls from deep within,
To where our journeys shall begin.

Fragments lost and memories found,
In every heartbeat, a new sound.
Threads of fate intertwine and flow,
Creating all we come to know.

From every star, a story told,
In whispers soft, the brave, the bold.
Both joy and sorrow, every shade,
Together form the life we've made.

The Art of Becoming

With each sunrise, a canvas waits,
Brushes poised beyond the gates.
Colors swirl in tender grace,
Life unfolds, a sacred space.

Shadows fade, as light breaks through,
Crafting dreams with every hue.
In the stillness, hearts ignite,
Chasing whispers, turning light.

Step by step, through storms and fears,
Forge ahead, through laughter, tears.
A sculptor's hands, we shape our fate,
In every choice, we learn, create.

The art of being, raw and pure,
In vulnerability, we find the cure.
For every tear, a lesson sown,
With every fall, we find our throne.

Embracing change, we dance and sway,
Through the moments, we find our way.
The masterpiece, a life set free,
A painted soul, eternally.

Journey to the Core

Across the plains and seas we roam,
Searching for a place called home.
The heart, a compass, leads us deep,
To inner realms where shadows creep.

Beneath the surface, treasures lie,
In whispers soft, the questions cry.
Each step we take, a story spins,
As silence speaks of where it begins.

Through forest green and mountains high,
In every tear, we learn to fly.
The core of self, a glowing light,
Guides us gently through the night.

In every stumble, grace unfolds,
As wisdom's voice begins to mold.
With every layer, truth we find,
A boundless journey, intertwined.

So onward now, embrace the quest,
For in the searching, we are blessed.
The journey's heart beats strong and sure,
A path of love, forever pure.

Milton Keynes UK
Ingram Content Group UK Ltd.
UKHW020047260824
447288UK00011B/301